WHAT NOT TO DRIVE

WHAT NOT TO DRIVE

**Richard Hammond
and Andy Wilman**

Weidenfeld & Nicolson
LONDON

First published in Great Britain in 2005
by Weidenfeld & Nicolson, a division of
the Orion Publishing Group Ltd
Orion House
5 Upper Saint Martin's Lane
London
WC2H 9EA

10 9 8 7 6 5 4 3 2

A CIP catalogue record for this book is available
from the British Library

ISBN-10: 0 297 84800 3
ISBN-13: 9 780 29784800 4

Printed and bound in Italy

www.orionbooks.co.uk

CONTENTS

PART TWO – Lifestyle Choices

INTRODUCTION

Stroll into your local newsagent and you'll find up to 100 car magazines on the shelves. That's a lot. Likewise if you're standing in a bookshop right now, pretending you're interested in this book until it stops raining outside, have a quick canter through the other literary works on cars. There'll be plenty: worthy manuals on doing up old Escorts; huge, glossy coffee-table jobs about the world's greatest supercars and nerdy masterpieces such as *Gearboxes of Bratislava* (1968–72). You'll find books on individual marques – Mini, Porsche, Ferrari – books on Damon Hill, books on Formula One and brainy books on the car industry. In short, the wealth of material written about the car is breathtaking, but no book until now has addressed the single most important issue facing motorists today, namely: What Your Car Says About You. If a book actually has addressed this, then we're sorry. But we don't think there is.

What Not To Drive is the style bible that helps you make the right car choice. And by 'right' we don't just mean the most reliable or best driving, but the car that's the coolest choice for you. This last point is very important. Cars today may not be the rusty old crocks they were 30 years ago, but just like your clothes and shoes, they speak volumes about the kind of person you are, and you still take a gamble every time you step into a showroom: Does that sports car make you superdude, or a prime-time cliché? Does a private plate say success or sadster? Are you going to choose your wedding car in haste and repent at leisure? Does your motoring life have to end when you buy a family car? These and many other questions will be answered in this important and groundbreakingish book.

PART
ONE

Chapter One

THE CELEBRITY FACTOR

The celebrity is now an important part of everyday life. You only have to look at the explosion of celeb magazines such as *Heat* and *Now* for proof. This really wouldn't matter if we were only interested in observing what they do – just exactly how Jude Law waits whilst his dog has a pee, for instance, or what specific change Ant and Dec put in a parking meter. But no, our fascination goes much deeper than mere star-gazing. What we're doing now is using celebs as lifestyle gurus, following their lead on how to dress and, inevitably, which car to drive.

Now aping dress sense doesn't really matter, because if you buy a gold lamé bikini in the hope of looking like Jodie Marsh, and then suddenly remember on the way home that you're a fireman from Hull, you've only wasted twenty quid. But using stars as a guide to cars is a very dangerous path to take, because famous folk are not necessarily a barometer for the correct choice of vehicle. Below are some examples to illustrate the point.

BAD CELEBRITY CAR CHOICES

HOLLYWOOD STARS AND THE TOYOTA PRIUS

Hollywood film stars by nature love a bit of drama, and they've reacted so over-dramatically to the stories that the world is about to be globally-warmed to death by the car that they've all gone out and bought Toyota Priuses. This £18,000 saloon is touted as the most environmentally friendly car you can buy, with a hybrid power unit that allows it to run on either a petrol engine or electricity, thus giving amazing fuel consumption. Some really big A-listers have been seduced by it too, including Leonardo DiCaprio, Daryl Hannah, Cameron Diaz and Harrison Ford. Unfortunately, though, you have to be DiCaprio to drive this car, because that's the minimum amount of charisma you'll need to counteract this car's plonker factor. It might be as quiet as a milk float, but it has the presence of one, too.

A Toyota Prius

Diaz sets off on milk round

SIMON COWELL AND THE MAYBACH

Cowell is a titan of television, earning £17 million alone last year from spouting his pithy put-downs, and, as we found when he came to the *Top Gear* show, he's also one of the most polite and charming people you could wish to meet. Unfortunately, though, when it comes to cars he cannot pick a winner with the same skill he demonstrates around pop singers. Cowell's car is a Maybach, which bills itself as the last word in luxury saloons and boasts club-class-style reclining seats for rear passengers. The top spec version costs £280,000 and offers two million combinations of colour, trim and equipment. Sadly, though, this is a truly, truly tasteless car, right up there with monogrammed swimming pools and walk-in wardrobes in the pantheon of vulgar greats. If you win the lottery, do not follow Cowell on car advice.*

* Simon Cowell has seen the light and now owns two Rolls Royce Phantoms instead of a Maybach.

CELEBRITY OVERKILL

This happens when celebrities swarm all over a particular car like velociraptors at its launch, and celebrity overkill turns what could have been a cool car into the most hackneyed accessory money shouldn't buy. A fine example of this is the BMW X5. In the early days, life was pretty good for this smart-looking Chelsea tractor, with a select band of stars – Madonna,

Kirsten Dunst, Steve Coogan – providing just the right amount of tasteful and cool patronage. But then a premiership footballer – usually Beckham – spots one and the next day the local dealer is piloting a brand spanking new model through the electric gates of his mock Georgian mansion. From there it's downhill all the way. Footballers are too thick to have an original thought, and a week later there's a squad of X5s parked up at the training ground. Legend has it that at one point

forty-eight premiership players had this particular BMW, but the decline doesn't end there, because once footballers give the car the nod, the D-list celebs come out of the woodwork, and before you know it H from Steps has one, as does Daniella Westbrook, and then just when you think it couldn't get any worse, Jade Goody is pictured in *Now* magazine loading up her X5 at Asda. It's at this point that the last of this BMW's dignity runs out. Once it's

been Goodyed, the car, like Burberry check, is officially naff. Car dealers should really learn from the X5 experience and make celebrities fill in a form before they sell them a car. Questions like: 'Have you ever appeared on a reality show?' 'Does the doorman at Chinawhite know you by name?' 'Have you spit-roasted a lap dancer with your mates in the last six months?' and 'Have you ever helped Abi Titmuss change batteries in her video camera?' would really go some way to sorting out the wheat from the riff-raff.

The previous examples will hopefully show that caution must be used when following the motoring tips of the stars. But there are some famous folk who make excellent ambassadors for the art of proper car choosing.

JAY KAY

The Jamiroquai frontman has the means to buy a £470,000 Ferrari Enzo, but it is the cheaper stuff in his car collection which reveals his style. His 1970s BMW 2002 is a classic example of Jay's taste. He always chooses with care, like a great chef taking time over even the most humble vegetable, and I would not hesitate to follow this man's recommendations.

SEAN CONNERY

The coolest old person on the planet drives a Land Rover Defender, which is appropriate given that this badly-built heap, with panel gaps wide enough to slide oil tankers through, is possibly the coolest car in the world. And if you need any more proof, his choice of vehicle is backed up by a plethora of global coolness, with other Land Rover owners including Bill Murray, Robin Williams, the Queen and Fidel Castro.

Connery with Aston Martin-shaped Land Rover

The Queen always wears a hoodie when she's nicking cars

ROGER MOORE

Connery may be the ultimate Bond, but on the suaveometer there is no more stylish an Englishman than Roger Moore. In fact his smoothness has made him one of the world's most famous actors even though he can't actually act. On the car front, Moore happens to be an exponent of the cheap heap. By this we mean a lowly car – old, battered and incredibly modest. Moore's particular machine is an old Renault 5, and what he's saying here is that he just doesn't care about his car, which is a very cool thing to do. However, be careful if you follow

Roger's route, because the car you don't care about has to be chosen carefully. The Renault 5 is OK, because small European superminis are intrinsically cool, but even the most stylish of stars cannot lift a shocker out of its cesspit. Bryan Ferry, for example, once owned a Toyota Previa. Enough said.

PAUL NEWMAN AND KRISTIN SCOTT-THOMAS

You'll be hard-pressed to find two more elegant film stars on the planet, and both of them drive Volvo estates. This again is another slab of stylishness from the Swedes, the sort of car that you own, rather than it owning you.

PUFF DADDY

In terms of being style gurus, the big R&B stars are the leading forces on the planet right now, and Puffy is still the daddy on this front. The man has studied carefully the dapper appearance of Sinatra and the Rat Pack, and consequently has given the customised Ferraris a body swerve in favour of a Rolls-Royce Phantom. This is a truly great car, and thanks to the power of bling, it's OK to be seen in a £220,000 Roller again, even if Bernard Manning still has his.

Puff Diddly in
Bentley Azure

CARS AND ROMANCE

Can the right car help you find true love? That's the question which has vexed automotive scholars for centuries, and which we will attempt to address in this chapter. The advice given in the following pages is mainly aimed at males, since it is still primarily they who have to do the chasing at the start of any courtship, and also it is predominantly men who are complete ocean-going car bores. This group really needs help because they in particular find it hard to combine their enthusiasm for, say, pre-war MGs, with their efforts to meet a loved one.

The first task in tacking this whole question of cars and romance is to ascertain just how important your choice of car is to a lady. To find the answer, we surveyed lots of women, asking them questions such as, 'Do you care what type of car a first date turns up in?' 'Would you go for a man on the strength of his car?' and 'Are you impressed by a flash car?' The results were very interesting. Of those surveyed, around about approximately somewhere in the region of 100 per cent replied, 'Not really,' or, 'No, not at all,' in response to the questions. Now obviously that's rubbish. They're just saying that. Of course they care what cars we drive, or what's the point of carrying on? It's like when women say they don't find burping attractive: you know that secretly they recognise it's an incredibly skilful art. So below is some handy advice on how to proceed along the road to romance, and if we've got

CARING TRENDY LEFTY WOMEN

This can cover anyone from a university student through to Germaine Greer via Gwyneth Paltrow and Stella McCartney. Kate Moss would be included in this bunch too, but it's probably best if we don't get too ambitious to start with. You really have to be careful with this type of lady, because these are the ones who will be least susceptible to any display of ostentation.

CHOICE OF CAR

Toyota Prius

A pretty miserable method of transport for anyone who likes soul in their wheels, but thanks to the patronage of Hollywood stars such as DiCaprio and Diaz, this ecofriendly hybrid-engined car is a good banker here. No premiership footballer will ever buy one.

Supermini

Avoid something like a hot Fiesta ST, with a big racing stripe down the middle – too vulgar and immature, and also steer clear of a Nissan Micra, which is too soppy. Instead, go for a Fiat Panda. This evokes a sense of knife-edge driving in Rome, or dashing across Milan during fashion week, and Italian city driving is a very passionate and sexy pastime. This little car also says you are completely secure about your masculinity.

Ford Fiesta ST

Fiat Panda

Old Crock

Trinny and Susannah themselves, the high priest-esses of advice on girl stuff, when questioned on the car issue both said the more knackered and dirty the car, the better. Apparently it shows that you're so relaxed and confident about your status that you don't feel the need to be propped up by expensive accessories such as a sports car. If you follow this strategy, though, make sure you get it right. Be careful to avoid cars that merely make you

Rover SD1

look poor and grim, such as an old 1992 Escort, and instead go for an old knacker with style, such as a Rover SD1, an original Mini or a Renault 5.

Classic Car

A classic says you don't run with the herd, and for specific recommendations refer to pages 83–93. Instead, we'll use the space here to talk about the art of accessorising your car to make you look an altogether more sensitive person. Stickers about worthy causes (preferably aged – give them a good rub with a teabag before putting them on) work well, plus some books on deep stuff – if you can find one about a man, preferably who's a woman, who restores a sideboard in Tibet and in the process of restoration rediscovers his soul, you're on the right track. Make sure the book is well thumbed, and give the spine a good few bashes on the steering column. Don't leave it obviously and prominently on the seat, because women will spot your plot. They'll always have a root around whilst you're paying for petrol anyway, so stick it in the door pocket. Finally, don't confuse sensitive with being a fairy. Make sure the car has a few faults up its sleeve, so that you can mend them in a manly manner, quickly and efficiently. Stuff that requires a tool or two, and some banging. Being at ease with both Racine and a wrench works wonders.

Citroen DS

HIGH-POWERED PROFESSIONAL

These women have seen it all. They've probably got their own Porsche 911 and they've heard all the TVRs being revved up in the underground car park, so avoid the clichéd sports cars. If you're going for expensive, then make sure it's discreet and tasteful.

TVR Sagaris

CHOICE OF CAR

Mercedes CL

This large German coupé is one of the most stylish-look-ing cars around. It's discreet, yet doormen at hotels know its worth. The CL is also reassuringly costly, with the cheapest one starting at £72,000.

Aston Martin DB9 Volante

Whereas Ferraris and Lamborghinis can be a turn-off, Aston Martins never ever suffer from such an affliction. In the wrong hands the Italians come across all suntan oil and eurotrash, but the Aston always has that classic Terry Thomas roguish charm.

Smart Roadster

This tiny two-seater may be hideously overpriced at £13,000–£15,000 for such a small-engined machine, but it has many compensating virtues regarding the business of courtship. For starters, it's so petite and unassuming that women won't think your penis is the size of a silicon chip, as so often happens if you roll up in a huge throbbing sports car. Secondly, it's also amazing fun to drive, but more importantly, it's amazing fun at low speeds, so you won't have to leave your dignity in a hedge whilst trying to impress with some spirited cornering. And finally, it's escapism. You get in this car, chuck the roof off and point the bonnet towards the countryside, and all your troubles just drift away.

GIRL ABOUT TOWN

This is the sort of normal person who's not as hung up about the world as the trendy lefty, and also not as mature, experienced or indeed as cynical as the career high-flyer. She's younger, and consequently her attitude to cars is so much more relaxed, and the key thing to remember is that she will like the car that she herself wants to own.

CHOICE OF CARS

Sports Cars

The BMW Z4 is a perfect example of what we mean. Girls love BMW Z4s and are therefore happy to see a chap turn up in one. They like the modernity of the slashed lines across the body-work, they like the speed and ease with which the roof comes down, and they will borrow it at every opportunity. Another recommendation in this area would be the Nissan 350Z, mainly because it's

BMW Z4

such a youthful car. With its California looks it could be the sort of machine that tears up the highway in *Fast and Furious*, and inside it's got a sound system to rival any club in Ibiza. More risky, but worth a punt, is the Mazda RX8. The drawback with this car is that all its interesting features are a trifle nerdy. Not many first dates will be interested, for example, in the oil consumption rate of its peculiar rotary engine. But it's quick, obviously sporty, and stands out from the crowd with its suicide doors and Japanese arcade game interior. Finally, you cannot ignore the new Vauxhall Astra VXR. With a 240-bhp turbocharged engine, it'll be monstrously quick, and, which is surprising for an Astra, looks unbelievably sexy as a 3-door.

Nissan 350Z

Superminis

If the girl in question is into the Max Power modifying scene, she'll naturally lean towards a Citroën C2 VTS or a hot Fiesta ST, both of which find favour amongst those who like to accessorise their cars with gusto. Moving into a slightly more mature category, the Mitsubishi Colt is a sound move, as is the new VW Polo GTi, on sale in late 2005 – with a 150-bhp 1.8-litre turbocharged engine it'll be fast, exciting, and the right VW is cool across all age barriers. Finally, and safest of all bets, the Mini.

Cars to avoid include the Toyota Yaris, which is retirement home transport, and the Ford Fusion and Mazda 2, because there's absolutely nothing cool about cars that are too tall.

The Mini – a banker

Citroen C2

CARS GIRLS DON'T LIKE MEN IN

Some cars are just completely wrong for men because they make you look either too butch, in a caveman way, or too gay, in a musical chorus-line sort of way. Here are a few examples:

Too Gay

Mercedes C Class Coupé

Renault Modus

Vauxhall Tigra

Daihatsu Copen

Nissan Micra

Peugeot 206cc

Peugeot 206 CC

Daihatsu Copen. Deary Me.

Mercedes C Class Coupé

Arnie and his Hummer

Mitsubishi Evo

Too Butch

Any Mitsubishi Evo
Hummer
Porsche 911 Turbo
TVR Tuscan
Any Caterham
MG SV

Form a queue, girls.

HANDY HINTS FOR CAR BORES
DEALING WITH NORMAL PEOPLE

Don't accessorise your car too enthusiastically. These feats of over-engineering do not impress in the same way that the Guggenheim Museum does.

If you feel compelled to show off your automotive knowledge, learn the difference between dull and interesting trivia.

DULL: 'Despite its overall low standard of workmanship, the Austin Allegro featured a hydrogas suspension system of considerable merit.'

INTERESTING: 'If you buy a Pagani Zonda, which is a beautiful Italian supercar, you get a pair of driving shoes made by the Pope's cobbler.'

If you've restored a classic car, don't, under any circumstances, bring out the photos which you've inevitably taken to document the restoration.

Don't offer to show her your shed on the first date. A switched-off lathe is never that interesting.

If you've been asked to 'look your best' for an evening out, that means leave behind, not put on, your badges from classic car rallies.

If she's into 'dogging' and you agree to go along, do try and comment on the actions of the other couples rather than snorting at their choice of car.

If the outcome of your first date is in the balance, you really won't swing it by showing her how far away you can stand from your car and unlock the doors with the remote plipper.

If you're lost, she honestly won't think you have an underwhelming penis if you stop and ask for directions.

Never, ever rely on car manufacturers' branded goods to woo a lady. Jaguar aftershave is a complete no-no, and if you come out of the bathroom sporting a Ferrari dressing gown, it won't make her suddenly forget that you drove her home in a Skoda Fabia.

Chapter Three
WEDDING CARS

It's the biggest day of your life; all your friends are there, you have lavished thousands of pounds and just as many hours on the event, you chose the flowers to match the brides-maid's bracelets, and your father's socks to match the cushions in the hotel reception. You fretted over getting the right weave in the paper for the invitations, agonised over what variety of kumquat to have with the starter, and auditioned two dozen harpists. So why is the wedding car always forgotten about?

The problem here is that the car is usually left to the bloke. The bride-to-be will research every item on her 'Wedding To Do' list more thoroughly than Watson and Crick looking for the structure of DNA. She will sift through a mountain of magazines, order samples, and then invite her friends round to clinic every single choice and decision. The bloke will clinic it with his mates in the bog, on the stag night. They'll agree that a white Roller is a wedding car and then it's one call to the Cheesy Daytime TV Wedding Co. and, hey presto, one wheezy old 1982 Roller pitches up outside your house on the Big Day, dripping oil and stinking of fags and dashboard polish.

Teenage Shotgun Wedding

Try to resist the temptation to be ferried to the church in a Subaru Impreza STi; it might impress your mates but, to be honest, you're unlikely to need a rally-bred four-wheel-drive system at a wedding. This is an opportunity to impress your new in-laws with your sense and wisdom beyond your years. Show them how frugal you can be too; dress your own car with white ribbons and put white sheets on the seats to cover some of the more dubious stains – amongst them probably the very ones that led you to the aisle in the first place.

Second Time Around

You're still young, you've found new love, you want to arrive in a sexy two-seater convertible to tell the world how good you feel. But you've both got kids from a previous marriage, and they've all got matching outfits for the big day, so you can't. That said, there's no need to turn up in a Renault Scenic full of broken biscuits and nappies either. A stretch limo would accommodate you and your newly combined brood, but see page 36 for reasons why this is not acceptable. You need a Maserti Quattroporte; it's beautiful, Italian, has loads of room inside and is very, very cool.

Old Timers

There are a few specific considerations here. You want something that's easy to get in and out of; it would be embarrassing for all concerned, and perhaps an untimely reminder of the limited future ahead of you, if you spend twenty minutes helping one another struggle out of the Lamborghini Murcielago you rather ill-advisedly ordered. Secondly, avoid the temptation to get anything that dates you. A vintage Roller would make the whole day look like a time-warp, people would be waiting for a mad professor to whisk you away in a

silver DeLorean covered in wires. Instead, go for something smart and modern. A Bentley Flying Spur would show that you are not afraid of technology, that you like luxury, and that you're happy to blow a few quid on yourselves, which should worry the inheritors, sorry, children.

CAR TYPES

The 'Classic'

Right, it's going to break down. Then you're going to stop being friends with whoever lent you their precious but knackered Triumph Spitfire, Healey or MGB. So if you're going to use something old, make sure it's hired, from someone you can sue. Once you've accepted that the bride will be, like, an hour late, rather than just the traditional pulse-quickening five minutes, and that her frock will be splattered with Duckhams, then she may as well be late in style. This leads inevitably to the Lamborghini Miura, one of the most beautiful cars ever made. No bride in history has ever used this as a wedding car, which is why you should.

Classics from the 1920s and 1930s

Great hunting ground here; cars from the early part of the century could be elegant and stylish with their upright postures and plush interiors, like the state rooms of great houses. The fact that they were rubbish at going along the road is neither here nor there, as you don't need to get the tail out in a wedding car. Go for something big, though; small cars of the period tended to be built around Elizabethans and no one wants to stand around embarrassed whilst

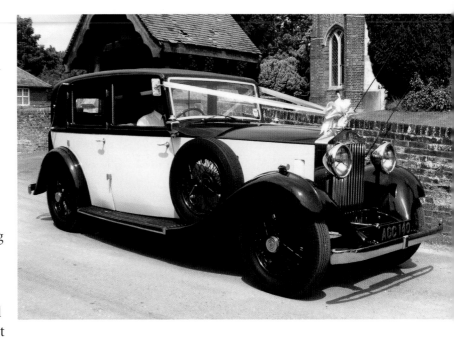

the bride struggles to get her backside through the door. Anything with a Rolls-Royce badge from this era is going to be good. Make sure the driver doesn't nod off though; he'll almost certainly be older than his car.

American

Tricky this, it smacks of a wedding 'theme': people might expect the bride and groom to break into a chorus of 'Mothers don't let your sons grow up to be cowboys' at the reception and stay away. But there is something glamorous about a giant 1950s American car. It can't be anything from later than 1965 – turning up in a tired old Trans Am with an Eagle on the bonnet is just wrong. The same goes for anything from the 1970s. Who wants their wedding cavalcade to look like a scene from the Blues Brothers? Well, quite a lot of people apparently, but they're sick. A 1958 Cadillac Fleetwood 60 Special Sedan will do nicely, and if it's raining you can get the whole family in it for the photographs. If you are sick in the head though, go for a 60s Dodge Charger, the muscle car of choice.

The Stretch Limo

The hen-night special is really never an acceptable option for wedding car duty. It will reek of stale Asti Spumanti, and there's every danger that one of you will recognise the leopard skin pants stuffed between the back seats and the drinks cabinet. The windows will be covered in boob-prints and the driver's phone stuffed full of 'candid' shots of his drunken passengers unwinding with friends, taken through the crack in the privacy screen. The limo worked in *Pretty Woman*, but let's not forget she was a prostitute. Not good on a wedding day.

Chapter Four
FAMILY CARS

It used to be simple. A family car was a grey saloon, usually a Vauxhall, with four doors and four seats. Not now though, it's like buying coffee; ask for one and you'll be hit with a thousand questions about what sort of sprinkles you want with that, and how would you like it stirred? Honestly, you've got MPVs, Mini-MPVs, Midi-MPVs, SUVs, estates, sports estates, off-road estates, sportswagons, off-roaders, soft-roaders, sports saloons and hatchbacks. Worse still, the good old stalwarts of the family car, Ford and Vauxhall, have been hit by 'Marks and Spencer syndrome'. Just as friendly old M&S has been flanked by discount Matalan and TK Maxx stores on one side and high street Armani stores on the other, so Ford and Vauxhall are challenged by cheap but useable stuff from the Koreans, like Hyundai and Kia, whilst premium stuff from Mercedes and Jaguar is suddenly becoming more affordable.

So consider this your guide through the bewildering choice of family cars. I have chosen the best and worst from five broad categories that really matter: 4x4, MPV, small MPV, estate and family hatchback.

4 X 4

There are those who condemn the off-roader as the wheels of Satan, intent on reducing the earth to ash and rubble, but they can make a lot of sense as a family car. Setting aside the off-road ability of these cars, which is, let's face it, only important to families living in lighthouses or Scottish bothies, a 4x4 offers a high seating position which the kids love, plenty of room on board, often for seven people, and they can easily pull a trailer full of kit or, if you absolutely must, a caravan.

BEST GO

Volvo XC90

The interior can be set up to seat seven in comfort, or fold the seats flat and you've space for a fridge freezer. You can specify DVD and gaming systems with separate screens for the kids in the back so they can play mega-robot-death III whilst Mummy dozes off with 'My Fair Lady' in the front and Daddy sits, red-eyed and alone, staring at the fogbound M4 and waiting for the fighting to start again to help him stay awake.

WORST **STOP**

Hyundai Santa Fé

There are three 4x4s in the Hyundai range, all of them pretty hopeless, and when a car-maker has to have three attempts at getting something right, that really should ring alarm bells. On the road, the Santa Fé drives like a waterbed, off-road it drives like someone let all the water out. Some people like the looks, but then some people fancy Rod Stewart, so what kind of guide is that? Plus someone is going to ask you what you drive and you're going to have to try to say 'Santa Fé' without sounding like someone in a camp musical. Leave well alone.

MPV

When they first arrived, people condemned them as nothing more than vans with windows, which they quite often were. The essential difference between an MPV and other cars, if you're interested, is the 'one-box' body construction. Basically, what this means is that the engine compartment, luggage compartment and the bit you sit in are all in one big box, rather than separated into three different little boxes, like in a saloon car. The result is much better use of the space, which means more room for everyone and the chance to include clever foldaway seats and lots of storage cubby holes for you to stow CDs and the kids to hide their fags.

BEST GO

Espace

it was the first European MPV and is still the best. Apart from anything else, it looks cooler than the rest, with spaceship-style wraparound door mirrors and lots of vents and slots to make it look like it goes faster than it really does. The interior is very alternative, with all the boring driving stuff like speedo and rev-counter dials kept to a minimum so that it feels like a big, mobile sitting room with air-conditioning. Not cheap, but worth the extra if you're lucky enough to have it.

WORST **STOP**

Galaxy

The Galaxy has been left behind, big time. Cars like Citroën's C8, with its clever sliding doors, make the big Ford look like a lumbering idiot from the Stone Age. It's fragile too, regularly coming in towards the bottom end of reliability surveys. You're going to look a proper nelly trying to explain away the temperamental and fragile nature of your car when it isn't an Alfa Romeo.

SMALL MPV

Like reality TV and text sex, this is not a concept that even existed just a few years ago. Credit must go once again to Renault for having a big part in inventing the concept, with their Mégane Scénic. It's essentially like taking a medium-sized hatch, popping a drinking straw up its exhaust and blowing gently to inflate it. The resulting bloated form makes for more space inside and some of the advantages of a full-sized MPV, without the parking challenges and with less of the 'I'm a family man/woman, ignore me, I'm boring and sexless' stigma attached.

BEST GO

Corolla Verso

Not so long ago, the Corolla was the most boring thing this side of window putty. As utilitarian as a frying pan with all the passion taken out, choosing to drive one was like telling the world that you line up your socks in the drawer, iron creases down the front of your jeans and organise your John Denver collection alphabetically. The clever Verso, though, is a far less shameful choice; it can carry seven people and has a flexible interior with seats that fold flat to make more luggage space. It drives well, looks OK, and though not cheap to buy, shouldn't cost a fortune to run. It's a Toyota too, so it should never break down, and if it does, your local dealer will send you his own head on a plate.

WORST **STOP**

Daewoo Tacuma

You wouldn't let the kids eat six kilos of jelly babies before setting off on a long journey would you? It would make them sick. Well, so will this horror. With a face like a melted welly, the hideous Tacuma lumbers into view, ruining the day of anyone unfortunate enough to see it. There are, apparently, some seats in there, and an engine is available, but really, do the world a favour, do not buy one of these unless you're going to use it in an experiment.

ESTATE CARS

For a while, it looked as though the estate car, with its sensible, practical approach, would vanish completely, beaten into submission by the more modern MPV. But no, it has clung on, continuing to offer its homespun virtues of a big loadspace, room for five – or occasionally seven – and the feeling that you're not at the wheel of something as big as a Scania truck. There are those for whom an estate car is actually a statement in itself; you can judge the success of an antique dealer by the year of his Volvo estate, and among posh people, the estate is an expression of a properly utilitarian approach to something rather vulgarly glamorised by the less tasteful. So I've subdivided them into two categories: Posh and Ordinary.

Posh Estate

BEST GO

E-Class

As posh as tweed trousers with paint on, the big Mercedes estate tells the world that you buy a car to carry stuff and people around in, and that you can't ruddy well be bothered to do so very often which is why you've always bought Mercedes estates. Some of them have been in the same family for generations; they are handed down together with the paintings that they find transported back to the ancestral pile.

WORST STOP

Audi A6 Allroad 4x4

Audi build some of the best estate cars available. This is not one of them. In fact it's really not quite clear what it actually is. The A6 Avant, upon which it is based, is excellent, so if you want an Audi estate car, you would have one of those. The extra couple of inches or so in height from the raised suspension are just enough to spoil the on-road manners but not enough to endow it with the ability to tackle terrain rougher than a bumpy garage floor. It's also expensive; you pay about £1500 for each extra inch of height compared to the ordinary A6 Avant.

BEST

Mondeo Estate

Okay, so your heart is not going to race when you stride towards it with the keys, but the Mondeo makes a fantastic estate. It looks good if you go for a dark colour and you can specify a red leather interior, which rocks. It's ready for duty too: the loadspace is truly enormous.

WORST **STOP**

Citroën C5

It is big, no one can take that away from it, but then so are some dog poos and is that necessarily a good thing? The C5 is also very, very ugly and a misery to drive. It's not so much what you'll be telling the world about yourself by driving around in one of these, it's what it might actually do to you over time, physically and mentally.

BEST **GO**

Ford Focus

Not surprisingly, this is one area of the market that is more than saturated with possibilities. Citroën's new C4, with its vibrating seat to warn you if you wander out of your lane, is great, Renault's Mégane can be pretty cool too. But in the end, with its huge choice of excellent engines, great handling and enormous interior space, the Focus is the one to go for, despite looking as bland as a box of polystyrene chips.

WORST

STOP

Fiat Stilo

It's getting very old now and well overdue being put out to pasture, so it comes as no surprise that the family Fiat falls down in a few areas: the way it looks, handles and rides, the engine, reliability, durability and depreciation. It is, in short, hopeless. Don't buy one to keep chickens in, let alone drive your family around.

CARS THAT SAY YOU'VE NOT GIVEN UP

Your first trip out in your new family car can be a bit daunting. You're sure people are looking at you differently, they know you're finished, your teeth have been pulled, wings clipped and other parts stuck in the blender for good. It doesn't have to be like this, at least not as far as your family car is concerned. There are choices out there that will accommodate your family and keep the blood coursing through your vein, er, veins.

Vauxhall Zafira Turbo

Heck, a year or so back the Zafira even starred in a TV ad featuring Boney M's 'Daddy Cool'. What further proof could you possibly need? It's quick, thanks to its turbocharged 2.0-litre engine, taking just 7.6 seconds to hit sixty and mash the Labrador against the back window. When you want to load it up with stuff – Boney M CDs, perhaps – you can fold the seats flat into the floor. If you're new to all this family stuff, remember to take the kids out first though.

Subaru Legacy Spec B

It looks very low-key, but in a cool, understated and stylish sort of way. But don't be fooled. Underneath, it's a bit of a beast with a 'rally-bred' four-wheel-drive system and a powerful engine. It's possible to go very fast indeed in this car, which should keep everyone quiet in the back. The answer to the perennial question, 'Are we there yet?' will probably be, 'Yes, but Daddy's got to go with the policeman now.'

Nissan Murano

Just look at it. Hardly boring is it? The Murano manages to look as good as a BMW X5 without bringing the footballer associations or the hefty price tag with it. If the kids aren't convinced by the way it looks, just tell them that it uses the same 3.5-litre as the Nissan 350Z sports car and watch them come round to it.

Land Rover Discovery

One of the few cars to weigh almost as much as the town it was built in, the new Discovery is a masterpiece of over-the-top engineering. Thanks to incredibly sophisticated computer control of the suspension, brakes and engine, the Discovery was built to conquer the Atlas Mountains before breakfast. Of course, you're really not likely to need to do that. In fact, so long as Solihull High Street can be conquered with ease, its off-road prowess is pretty much irrelevant, but it's great to know that it can do it. For adventurous families living in log cabins on snowy mountainsides with bears as pets and racoon hats, it's an absolute must-have.

SCHOOL RUN

With parenthood comes a whole bunch of responsibilities, but principal amongst them is not making a total arse of your offspring every time you drop them off at the school gates. Let them be seen by their ten-year-old friends climbing out of Dad's Kia Magentis and they will grow up to be murderers, simple as that. If you do nothing else, as a mother or father, you absolutely must consider your child first when you next buy a family car. Their future depends on it. Of course, what you absolutely must not do is leave it up to them to choose. These then are the cars that your kids would choose if given the chance…

Mitsubishi Evo VII MR FQ-400

Look, Mum; it's got four seats, four doors and a boot. It's a sensible family car. Of course it is. Couple of points, though. Contrary to what you might be told by your precious little one, the carbon fibre wing is there for good reason and it's not to hang your blazer on whilst you check you've got your homework in your satchel. Under that louvred bonnet with its flaring intakes is a 400-bhp turbocharged psychopath of an engine. With a rally-bred four-wheel-drive system and more computer gubbins than your teenager's bedroom, it can hit sixty in 3.5 seconds and fuel consumption is rumoured to get down to about 4 mpg if you drive hard, which you will because it is utterly, completely impossible to resist.

Porsche 911

It's always been the supercar you can use every day, Dad, so why not… Well, once again, it ticks the right boxes. There are four seats in there, though you will struggle to get the children in the back past the age of three…

days. The leather interior won't take kindly to crayon embellishments but the whole thing should still be as tough as heck. Pulling up outside the school gates and strolling nonchalantly round to the back of the Porker to retrieve your sports kit from the boot, only to open the lid and reveal the engine lurking there will kind of hurt the credibility you gained by pitching up in it though, so be warned.

Mazda RX8

Again, the seats number four, only this time you'll find they really are big enough to put people in, not just Ken and Barbie. Better still, there are four doors. Thanks to the clever backwards-opening rear ones, no one will ever know it's not a two-door coupé. It's good value too, and being a Mazda, should be reliable. There is a slight problem; actually, make that a big one. The engine. It's a rotary one, a rare thing, and manages to make lots of power from just a small 1.3-litre capacity. But it's called a Wankel. Nuff said, kids.

Mercedes G55 AMG G-Wagen

Ooh crikey, you can see why the little darlings would want to be seen clambering out of this baby on their way to Monday morning assembly. Who in their right mind would mess with them? It's like having your very own four-wheeled bouncer in a dinner suit. The big Merc is based on a 25-year-old military vehicle, so it can walk the walk as well as talk the off-road rufty-tufty talk. The huge V8 engine bellows through side pipes, it's got more power than a Porsche 911 turbo and the door sills have 'AMG' on them, illuminated in blue; very, very cool. The kids arriving at school in this will almost certainly go on to lead nations, set up multinational corporations and become dictators on small, tropical islands.

Chapter Five
FASHION CARS

Fashion cars create a very dangerous and seductive trap. These are cars that make a massive impact when they hit the streets, and everyone talks about them, then Sienna Miller pops up in *Heat* trying to park one and the next minute smug dealers are waving a year-long waiting list in your dejected face.

The main reason why fashion cars hit the spot with such comet-like ferocity is that they look so striking at birth – and that very issue is the nub of the problem. The clue is in the word – they're fashion items, and like fashion items, they age in half an hour. So two things can go wrong. You buy one immediately, but then everyone gets one and unless you have a sign on the top saying, 'I bought mine first,' you soon look like a cock. Or you buy one a bit later, at the same time as the herd, in which case you instantly look like a cock.

How to Spot a Fashion Car

Most fashion cars are retro-themed. What this means, according to designers from car companies, is: 'Drawing on the styling heritage cues of a particularly iconic car or styling era to evoke the classic bloodline inherent in the marque.' Or you could call it bone idleness.

The main culprits of this black polo-neck work shyness are the VW Beetle, the Chrysler PT Cruiser, and the Mini. But as with all matters fashion, there are some timeless classics in amongst the Top Shop tops, so take a look at my handy Buy It or Bin It chart to guide you through these stormy waters.

VW Beetle

BIN IT

This had a massive impact, it has to be said, when it first came out in the mid nineties, but the impact was so colossal in the first five minutes of its life that buying one now is a humungous missing-of-the-boat moment, like going to the pub today dressed – without a fancy dress party to go on to later – as a member of Spandau Ballet. Also, given that this car is about posing, it has to be said you do look a dick from side on at traffic lights, due to the comedy driving position. Worse still, from the front it looks like a simpleton smiling. The convertible version of 2003 did pep things up briefly, but the folded roof at the back looks like you're taking a carpet to the tip. Another problem: the car itself is a joke. It's not an original car, but simply an old Golf with a frock on, and a zillion times more expensive. On that point though, it does at least evoke the heritage of its predecessor, the sixties Beetle, in that it too was a shit car. A million hippies may have bought one, but tell me, when did you last turn to a beatnik for advice on consumer goods?

Chrysler PT Cruiser

BIN IT

Retro models only make sense if they ignite sparks of emotion by performing a sort of automotive regression therapy that takes us back to memories of the original: you owned one first time round, or were driven in one as a kid, or had the toy, etc. On that basis a car modelled on fifties American Hot Rods, as the PT Cruiser is, doesn't make any sense over here. We simply don't have the culture to back it up. People from Scunthorpe don't appear in Springsteen lyrics. They don't race between 53rd and Madison on a last-chance power drive, and nor do they drive a Chevy to the levee or know the way to San José. Instead, they drive Fiestas, eat kebabs and vomit over police dogs on Friday nights. So given the massive gulf between the cultures, the Cruiser has no place here.

That's no loss, actually, because in engineering terms it's a very average car, and worse still, it's actually a family car trying too hard to be cool.

Mini
BUY IT

This is a tricky one. After several years on sale this car remains in such high demand that it's bullet-proof to criticism, and it's easy to see why: it's a great car to drive, it looks superb both inside and out, and without doubt it would have succeeded on its own merit even without the pedigree of the original to back it up. However, there is a problem, particularly in the London and Surrey area, where a large estate agency firm uses them as their workers' run-abouts, decked out in the most teeth-grating livery yet seen on a company car. I'm afraid this has blown Mini ownership for normal citizens in these vicinities, so if you want one badly, you'll have to sell up and buy a house elsewhere. Try Foxtons.

Mazda MX5

BUY IT ✓

This little roadster is based spiritually on the 1960s Lotus Elan that Emma Peel drove, but it's been around so long now – over a decade in fact – that it's almost a classic in its own right. It's been through its 'must-have' fashion moment and come out the other side unscathed, largely due to the fact that when all the hype died away, you were still left with a great car of amazing substance. It's like Leonardo DiCaprio: *Titanic* made him a megastar pin-up, but underneath there's always been a brilliant actor. And today, even though it's over ten years old and loads of rivals have snapped at its heels along the way, the MX5, with its snorty exhaust, snick snick gearchange and incredible handling, still remains the best small roadster money can buy.

Emma Peel in Lotus Elan

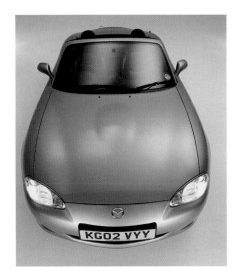

New Mazda MX5

Jaguar S-Type
BIN IT

Possibly the ultimate example of car-designer bone idleness. The starting point for this retro venture was the Mk2 Jaguar, that timeless classic much loved by robbers and a cop, old Morse himself. Now unlike, say, the Beetle, the Mk2 is a machine of such beauty that it should be left alone for posterity, but the Jag men charged with creating the S-Type dived in anyway, and presumably just after they'd started there was a power cut, but they carried on working away in the dark. That can be the only explanation for the eyesore we now see on the roads today, which looks like it could have been the original, but has sort of melted in the sun. Shame really, because underneath the diesel engine is a corker, and it's actually a brilliant car to drive. If you do buy one, then at least you won't have to look at it from the outside.

Mercedes SL

BUY IT

Where Jaguar went wrong, Mercedes has got it exactly right with the SL which, when it went on sale in 2002, became the most desirable car on the road overnight, with a waiting list of almost two years. The trick they pulled off was to use just the right amount of retro. Instead of smearing it on with a trowel like Jaguar did, they borrowed just a side air vent from a classic SL, and a sloping line here and there, and hey presto, just enough clues to say this car had devilishly handsome parents.

Ford GT

BUY IT

This car is meant to pay homage to the great GT 40, which found fame by slaying Ferrari at Le Mans four times on the trot in the late 1960s. The modern-day road car could so easily have been a feeble *Stars in Their Eyes* tribute, but underneath the bodywork there is, like the modern Mini, a great car in its own right. Its massive 5.4-litre muscle car engine is bulked up even further with the help of an Eaton supercharger, making it good for a top speed of well over 200 mph. Just one thing. Ignore the 'Buy It' tag at the top. There's only 28 slated for the UK and all are sold.

ART CARS

These are cars which, bizarrely, seem to follow an art movement as inspiration for their styling.

Chrysler Crossfire
BIN IT

There's an art-deco theme running through this American coupé, conveniently relating it to its bricks and mortar namesake, the Chrysler Building in New York. Sadly the building itself would make a more comfortable form of transport than this wretched lash-up of old German components.

Polo Harlequin
BIN IT

A close disciple of the art movement founded by St Wystan's Nursery toddler playtime paint group. As regards whether you should be seen in one, you can probably work this one out for yourself.

Chapter Six

PRIVATE PLATES

The DVLA makes £77m a year from selling us number plates with collections of letters and numbers that even if you squint, stand at a distance and put a hand over one eye, look nothing like the words they tell us they spell. This shameful statistic says more about Britain than football hooliganism, car crime or school bullying. It is a trade based entirely upon snobbery and gullibility.

They don't work. How many words in the English language use the number '4'? None. Neither is a '6' really a 'G' or a '5' an 'S'. Putting the bolts that hold the plate on in strategic places to break numbers or letters up and make them say what you want doesn't work either. So give up. Car traders think they are classy, enough said.

To make it easier to avoid buying one even by accident, I have divided them into categories:

The Unbelievably Expensive Plate

These are the very few that actually do spell out the owner's name or initials, followed by the number 1 or 2. Still unforgivable, and made worse by the knowledge that the owner can afford to blow squillions on the plate as well as a car that costs as much as a house. Usually to be found adorning Range Rovers, Bentleys, Rollers and Jaguars.

The Pompous Plate

This spells out the owner's initials and then a random number for which they will have made up a reason. For example, DTO 432. David Thomas Oliver will tell you proudly that he's actually got 432 fence posts outside his house. Generally fitted to large executive cars.

The Comedy Plate

There was only ever one truly funny number plate; it was PEN15 and was apparently taken out of circulation years ago. People still try though, imagining that they have spelt out 'Big Ted' when they really haven't. These can be found on anything which the owner feels is 'wacky', so look out for pink Suzuki Vitaras and any red car with big spots painted on to make it look like a ladybird.

The Twee Plate

Husbands and wives with 'His' and 'Hers' plates are the obvious examples, but others include cutesy little tags like 'Mum' and 'Debs', together with yet another entirely random number which will have been given a spurious significance by the owner displaying it. These are usually found on lukewarm hatches, small Japanese off-roaders and two-seater convertibles like the MX5.

The Meaningless Plate

The most annoying of all, the word supposedly spelled out is broken up with numbers and other letters to make a meaningless jumble. You do not, for instance, spell 'Magic' with a '4' popping up in the middle and a '6' instead of a 'c'.

Chapter Seven
THE RULES OF COOL

In the twenty-first century, this chapter probably contains the most important advice of all when deciding what to drive. You see, if this book had come out thirty years ago, when many automobiles were shoddily assembled by workshy lefties in the Midlands, the advice in it would have been pertinent, meaningful, life or death stuff: which cars had brakes made of pig's liver, or which ones cheekily rearranged themselves into a pile of rust whilst you dashed into the shops.

But today, although there still are some pretty vile driving experiences lurking in the show-rooms, most cars are, in the main, OK. They don't rust, the windows come with electricity, an airbag is stuffed in there somewhere, etc. Some of them might come bottom of a reliability survey, or whatever, but even the crap performers score over 75 per cent, which was a First when I was at university. There's plenty of heart surgeons out there who got 60 per cent in their exams, you know.

So if driving performance and reliability are no longer the make or break issues they used to be, we need another yardstick against which to make our purchase, and that yardstick is cool-ness basically – how cool is my car? What does my car say about me?

It's a bit like clothes, really, and naturally, as with all matters involving style, it's more complicated than you might think. It's not just a case of looking at what 50 Cent's bought and doing the same, because this would be silly if you're a rural vet. But the following handy hints will help lay out the basic ground rules to put you on the cool/uncool wavelength.

Forget About How Good the Car Is

This is the first and most important rule. A car's coolness or uncoolness has nothing to do with how quickly it goes round a corner or how well it's nailed together. The Chrysler 300c, for example, has the driving dynamics of a donkey, but no car around matches it for sheer presence. Conversely, the BMW 3-Series is often voted best driving saloon by anoraks, yet every close and crescent in Milton Keynes is infested with them. Not cool.

Chrysler 300C

Beware Supercars and Sports Cars

An easy trap to fall into. Ferraris, for example, are seen as the pinnacle of automotive erotica, and in engineering and pedigree terms, indeed they are. But who drives them? Middle-aged timber-yard tycoons from Surrey, that's who. Same story, unfortunately, with TVRs – the chariot of unimaginative city boys.

3 Series – not tacky at all.

Ignore Price Tags

This is the flip side of the supercar rule. Money doesn't really matter in the topsy-turvy world of cool. It's the man walking down the street with a baby syndrome. Men may think this to be an irksome, middle-aged predicament, but women who have their Mills and Boon goggles on see a hunk rescuing a puppy from a burning house. Likewise, cheap cars are fine – small European superminis in particular.

It's Different for the Sexes

A girl looks cool driving a TVR, whereas a man does not. A girl looks cool in a Mitsubishi Evo, whereas a man does not. A girl looks cool in a Smart Roadster, whereas a man does not. Sadly though, it doesn't work the other way round. There are no cars that men look cool in, that girls don't, if you get my drift.

Cars Change Status

This is dealt with more thoroughly in Fashion Cars (pages 58–67), but basically, be aware that some cars can start off cool, and then slide into Gary Barlow status as time goes on. Usually it's because they're too popular. Come in Audi TT, your time is up.

Colour Matters

Some colours are overdone and render a car uncool. Silver is a definite problem child here. People buy cars in silver because they think it's subtle and understated, a bit of Armani rather than Versace. They are actually trying to be cool, but it's about as original as exposed brick in loft apartments. White is due for a big comeback.

Never Discuss Cool with Salesmen

Just don't even go there, as they have no idea what you're on about. These are the people, remember, who try and entice customers into their showrooms by covering the forecourt with balloons. I ask you, what businessman in his forties, driving home, thinks: 'Yes, balloons! I *must* go in there and get a new Audi.'

Accessorising Doesn't Work

Trinny and Susannah may be able to liven up a drab twinset with the deft addition of a belt or a feathery thing or whatever, but sadly you cannot accessorise a car into cool. A Citroën C5 garnished with 20-inch alloy rims will not suddenly become the ride of choice for 50 Cent. It will merely be a Citroën C5 with wheels that wish they were somewhere else. The only useful accessory is dirt: not washing a Ferrari means you don't care, which is a good signal to send out.

Citroen C5

Dirty is good. Apparently.

Ignore Racing Drivers

These are the gladiators of the PlayStation era, a small band of warriors happy to go wheel to wheel at 200 mph on the straights of Monza. And because their day job is so unbelievably glamorous, you'd be forgiven for thinking they have something to contribute to the world of cool. Not so, as the pictures demonstrate. Here you have a film star playing at being a racing driver, and the real racing driver, as you can see, is not quite so stylish.

These rules may at first seem hard to follow, but persevere, and like the Force in *Star Wars*, one day you will just 'feel' them.

TOP THREE
COOLEST CARS

Land Rover Defender
It was around before the printing press, and you could run a canal boat down the panel gaps, but this car is utterly fit for purpose, and doesn't care what the world thinks.

Aston Martin DB9
The shape is right and the noise is definitely right. One of the very few supercars that don't make the owner look like a tool.

Alfa Romeo Brera
This showers its owner with exactly the same sparkle dust as the Aston does, but for a quarter of the price at £25,000.

TOP THREE UNCOOLEST CARS

BMW 316 Compact
The whole car smells of desperation. You crave a 3-Series, but can only afford the cheapest one. It's like ordering one caviar egg. Just walk away – you'll find a lot more happiness in other cars. They're as common as muck anyway.

Perodua Kenari
Just look at it. A unicycle offers more dignity, and is faster.

Lexus SC430
Desperately ugly from the front or back, which is unsurprising, since the back looks the same as the front. Lower the electric hood, and step into a world of wood from a 1950s council flat.

Chapter Eight
CLASSIC CARS

As a reader of this book, you are probably not a dyed-in-the-wool, fully-paid-up flat-capped member of the classic car fraternity. You are more the type who arrives at work and announces that you saw a...

Well, trust me on this one, don't do it. You are wandering wide-eyed and innocent into a minefield. You are popping 'over the top' of a First World War trench wearing a hi-vi fluorescent vest to go and buy some cowbells.

I know, it sounds perfect: why buy a boring old Ford Mondeo when for the same money you could drive around in an Alfa Romeo Montreal with a V8 engine and body styled by legendary designer Bertone? Well, for one thing you won't actually be driving around in it. You'll be sitting by the side of the road in it, wishing you had a Mondeo. And then there's the money; it might have cost less to buy, but whilst a Mondeo will need servicing every 10,000 miles, most classic cars need to be pretty much rebuilt every couple of hundred yards, which is expensive. And then there's the experience of actually driving it. Even on the smallest modern cars, we take for granted features like brakes that work, steering that lets you point the car where you want it, and suspension that keeps the wheels on the ground and stops your teeth shattering if you go over a manhole cover. Not so in classic stuff. Many of them are pretty much undriveable in today's traffic.

But despite all of this, it is possible to get it right, as long as you avoid the major pitfalls.

THE GREATS

There are those classics that have been elevated to a status that puts them beyond mere cars. They are icons, images familiar to generations of people who have never even stood next to one, let alone driven one. But they are dangerous territory for you. Think of the kind of people who like classics. Do they strike you as the type to take the easy route? No, in going for classic cars they have already made it plain that they like things to be tricky, unreliable and complicated. The cars that they prize above all others, then, must exhibit these traits in abundance – more in fact than all other classics. If these cars are the most classic of classics, then doesn't that ring alarm bells with you?

Jaguar E-Type

What more is there to say about someone who drives an E-Type? They enjoy a good moustache, they almost certainly have a selection of tweed hats in a variety of styles, they wear driving gloves and have never actually lived in a glamorous bachelor pad in Chelsea, despite trying to convince you that they have. It looks curvaceous, but the E-type was endowed with the aerodynamic qualities of a cowshed.

Aston Martin DB5

Yes, it is indeed a beautiful thing. But it is also ruinously expensive to buy and run, and who wants to spend their entire life talking to strangers about James Bond?

Citroën DS

Star of a thousand French films in which hollow-cheeked men in big coats fail to make love to thin, pale girls on bicycles, the DS is one of the most glamorous and beautiful cars ever made. It is also one of the most complex. At a time when other cars were as simple as bar stools, the DS came along with its hydraulic suspension, power steering, directional headlamps and disc brakes and simply blew everyone's minds. Today it will just blow all of your money keeping it going. It's strictly one for millionaire poets with engineering degrees.

AVOID

AMERICAN CLASSICS

It's easy to be seduced by the idea of an American classic; they are huge, have great big engines and can be very cheap. But be warned, it's not a good idea. In America, classic cars are only ever driven by murderers and ladies tend to avoid their company. For that reason, quite a few of them end up over here, where they are also driven by murderers.

Recent American Classics

Do not bother with any mainstream seventies stuff; it drives badly, looks awful and rusts so fast it fizzes like an Alka-Seltzer in the rain.

1950s American Classics

Fifties American cars look magnificent; huge, finned land yachts built to waft across entire states at a steady fifty miles an hour. But there's the clue. They weigh as much as oil tankers and are designed to proceed in a straight

line for thousands of miles. Some of them will take a hundred miles or so to come to a stop. Besides which, given their enormous size, you would have to move into the garage with the family and keep the car in the house.

1960s American Muscle Cars

Muscle cars are another example of great American excess. Build an enormous car and then decide it has to be a sports car, so fit it with an engine big enough to power a comet around the universe. Then wonder why the brakes, steering and prehistoric suspension are not up to the job of keeping the thing on the road. Muscle cars really are the preserve of the truly stupid. Only people desperate to draw attention to themselves in a spectacularly knuckle-headed way would choose to drive one. I got mine last year and it has proved itself to be every bit as hopeless as I expected. I have fitted modern brakes

and updated the suspension, but I still have to get out and put chocks under the wheels in an emergency. It uses fuel at only a slightly slower rate than I can put it in, and the engine is so loud that after a long journey my eardrums are hanging out of my ears like socks and I have to jam them back in with my thumbs. You'd have to be nuts to get one.

BRITISH STUFF FROM THE 1960s OR EARLIER

There are some great cars from back then, but today they are getting seriously vintage, which means they won't work. But mechanical fragility is not the real issue here; it's the lifestyle. You will have to join a club, which means spending precious spare time going to club meets and rallies, which will take ages because your car will break down on the way, and then, whilst you're at the side of the road trying to repair your 1962 Woodley-Armstrong Trumpet Special, or whatever, you will have to talk to the old giffer who emerges from a hedge to tell you that they don't build 'em like they used to, and in his day they could fix a broken wheel with bits of stick and re-grind the crank by the roadside with Marge's old tights and a couple of hair grips. Worse still, you will one day become Club Secretary which will mean writing a quarterly 'magazine' all about breaking down in an MG in Switzerland, and once a year you'll have to sit in a smelly old frame tent in a field in Devon for the annual club meet at which elderly men with dicky bladders stand around recalling fondly the times and places their old girls have broken down whilst the old girls they married sit and bicker about their children's successes and failures.

Triumph TR5

You will have to buy and wear a fake Second World War fighter pilot's jacket which is completely unacceptable. Youths in lukewarm hatches will leave you for dead at the lights and it will rust faster than you can weld it.

Morris Anything

For God's sake, they had names like 'Bullnose', 'Oxford' and 'Standard'. Not really very cool, is it?

AVOID

MGB

The MGB was, in its day, an outdated piece of nostalgic old junk. Today then, it's beyond belief that anyone would want to pull on their string-backs and clog up the country lanes in one. The best thing, if you must have one, is to buy one with a sunroof, put it at the bottom of the garden and plant a tree in it.

Rover P5

The height of luxury in the 1960s, which means it has carpet not lino on the floor and the windows open. Why do you want to look like a 1960s civil servant, anyway? You'll have to wear a bowler hat and carry an umbrella everywhere.

THE 1970s REVIVAL

Don't get misled into thinking that cars from the seventies were any good. They weren't. Built from old biscuit tins, they were flimsy, unreliable, unsophisticated and slow. But they are definitely cool today. For a third of the price of a small modern hatchback, you could be grooving around in a Granada like the one that starred in *The Sweeney*. It won't be much fun to drive, but you will look very, very cool. Their mechanical simplicity means that whilst yes, they absolutely will break down, they shouldn't cost a fortune to stick back together again.

Ford Granada 3.0s

Has to be in 'Roman Bronze' with a velour interior. You don't have to go fast to get the tyre-screeching sounds off the telly, 'cos the handling is crap.

Original Opel Manta A

First seen in 1970, the shark-nosed Manta, with its elegant round tail lamps, was a handsome car that would look very sleek and cool today. Shame they were all swept away as piles of rust years ago.

Original Mini

Not strictly a car of the seventies, but the early ones had head-light dipswitches on the floor and wouldn't go over forty, so forget those and get one from the seventies. There's such an air of authenticity about the original Mini, you can sneer at estate agents in their fake BMW Minis that cost ten times what yours cost and are only twenty times faster, thirty times more comfortable and a hundred times safer.

GO FOR...

Maserati Ghibli

There's one in *Kill Bill*. Enough said. It will ruin you financially, but who cares?

Rover SD1

The SD1 replaced the matronly P6 and is still a good-looking car with the added advantage of a 3.5-litre V8 thrumming away.

Rover SD1

Porsche 928

The 928, with its largely aluminium body, 4.5-litre V8 engine and squidgy rear end in place of a bumper was the car that Porsche wanted to make, not those silly rear-engined 911s. It's still quite good to drive today and definitely a bit of retro cool.

Porsche 928

Mercedes 280SL

Verging on being a bit obvious, but a good one still carries a lot of credibility. The last of the 'Pagoda roof' ones look the prettiest. People will assume you run an advertising agency.

Mercedes SL

1980s CARS

GO FOR...

As a general rule, if the music comes back, then so do the cars. Whilst people aren't yet wandering the streets in baggy shirts and making doe-eyes through a floppy fringe, the eighties have enjoyed a bit of a revival so it's a safe bet to consider the cars. Not only that, but eighties cars aren't really that old, and as they come from a time before the nanny state throttled all of the fun out of most things in life, some still have that snarly edge of danger missing from a lot of safety-obsessed modern stuff. This is actually a great way of getting performance on the cheap.

Peugeot 205 1.6 GTi

Legendary hot hatch from the days when hot meant it could hurt you. Drive one of these and impress people with your bravery.

VW Corrado

A very classy car, discreetly good looking and still a real performer, the Corrado didn't stick around for long, so it has a special rarity appeal.

Audi Quattro Coupé

Remind impudent Mitsubishi Evo drivers just how this whole four-wheel drive on the road thing started. An Audi Quattro will mark you out as a discerning driver with an appreciation of the real thing.

Ford Sierra RS Cosworth

Any image problems can be dismissed as irony, which will leave you to revel in the raw performance of the thing. It might not be subtle but it goes like hell and you will get a lot of respect, from certain quarters of society anyway.

Porsche 911 Turbo

Why not do the eighties thing property, pull on your braces and go for the full Athena poster Turbo Carrera in Guards red? Long live capitalism. It will at some point spit you off a roundabout and up a tree, but assuming you survive, you'll almost certainly pull in hospital when you show them the photos.

DICTATORS' CARS RULE

They may not feature on many Christmas card lists, but one thing they know about is getting the right set of wheels. In fact, through the decades, dictators have shown a good grasp of style; they have always had the best clothes. Watch any democratically elected prime minister step off the plane and you will see a sour-faced man or woman in a sombre grey suit. Now watch a grinning dictator emerge and you can hardly see them for gold braid, medals, fancy hats and lanyards. The same goes for the car. Whilst Harold Wilson was lighting up his pipe in the back of a Rover P5, Idi Amin was lording it up in the back of a magnificent Mercedes 600 Pullman. Pick a dictator's car and you can't go far wrong.

Of course, you have to bear in mind that if you do follow a dictator's lead in your choice of car, it will have to be a Mercedes. As you can see from this list:

Kim Jong-Il	Fleet of Mercedes S-Class limos
Bashar Assad	1954 Mercedes convertible and fleet of Mercedes limos
Daniel Arap Moi	Mercedes SL and fleet of Mercedes limos
Idi Amin	3 Mercedes 600 limos
Augusto Pinochet	Mercedes limo
Hirohito, Mubarak and Tito	Mercedes 600 Pullman
Chairman Mao	Mercedes 600 Pullman

There are very few dictators who don't drive Mercedes. King Mswati III of Swaziland is more of a BMW man. He has a fleet of ten BMW 7-Series, but then even he also has a Maybach 62, which is a Mercedes. When Augusto Pinochet was attacked in 1986, in amongst his convoy of Mercedes were a beige Ford Granada and an Opel. They both bought it, whilst Pinochet got away in his, you guessed it, Mercedes.

PART TWO

LIFESTYLE CHOICES

In this section we'll be looking at lifestyles, be it a profession or a type of person, and suggesting, telling them actually, which cars to avoid and which ones to go for. The choices of cars will be based on a mix of two main criteria (a) whether I think they're any good on merit, e.g. looks, driving experience, and (b) how they perform under the Rules of Cool.

Sadly there isn't space here to cover every profession or lifestyle, but there should be at least one category that comes close to you and your lifestyle. Sort of. For example, the suggestions for Lottery Winners work equally well for self-made Northern businessmen; IT Consultant covers plenty of people with technological-ish jobs, and Sales Reps can also cover people who work in an office with a tie on.

THE LOTTERY WINNER

The first rule is: do buy something that costs a few quid. There's nothing more annoying than people who become overnight millionaires and then declare they'll keep their K-reg Transit. You've got the money, go and live the dream for all of us. Being rich is quite a tricky business, and you might feel in a bit of a no-man's-land between your old poor friends and your new rich ones, so the knack is to buy something your mates won't get the urge to key, and yet makes sense in well-heeled company. Another tip: don't buy whatever your favourite footballer drives. The odds are it'll be vulgar or he'll have sold it for something else by the time you get yours home.

Cars to go for:

Rolls-Royce Phantom

This is a proper luxury car with old-money attitudes. There are few buttons to press which is odd in modern times, but that's the point: gentlemen shouldn't have to work, so let the car do things for you. Even the rear door closes electronically if you can't be bothered to do it yourself. Inside it's a world of art-deco lamps, real wood, and leather from eighteen hides. Also there's nothing so grubby as a rev counter; instead you get a 'power reserve' dial. Lovely, and a snip at over £200,000.

Aston Martin DB9

Like the Phantom, everything about this car smells of discreet British luxury rather than
Premier League vulgarity. Your old friends will applaud your choice too, as Astons are beyond
class issues: everybody from any background, of any age, loves them. And unlike previous
Astons, this one is not a bodge-up, but a hi-tech wonder car with stunning looks and a
ferocious V12 engine. Every detail, from the crystal engine ignition button to the inlaid
modern woods, reeks of discreet modern good taste. Your 200 mph car will also only cost
around £100,000, half the price of the Phantom.

Cars to avoid:

Lexus SC430

Somebody at the golf club will recommend one of these sooner or later – fifty grand, big V8, trick folding roof, blah blah – but please, just don't. This car has its own special place in our 'Uncoolest Cars' list, partly because it's so ugly and mainly because of the interior, where the wood panelling is about as genuine as the smiles from EuroDisney workers. On top of that the ride is rubbish. Hollywood plastic surgeons go for this car. Enough said.

Skoda Superb

Now, if you're finding the leap to a life of luxury a bit daunting, you might be tempted by the Skoda Superb. It's a logical thought: the badge definitely isn't posh in a Paris Hilton way, your friends will feel you haven't 'lost touch', and yet because the car is called a 'Superb' and is the flagship of the fleet, it still acknowledges your new status. No. This is like putting stone-cladding on Windsor Castle. The only time you should step in a Superb is when you need a minicab to take you to the Heathrow terminal for Barbados.

POOR, BUT WANT A NEW CAR

It's a trait that's peculiar to the British, but we like new cars. Maybe it's because of the ingrained Keep Up With The Joneses snobbery that was nurtured by our old number plate system, whereby your car's newness was there for all the neighbours to see. Or maybe it's the salesman's flowers, or that funny new car smell, a mixture of shop floor, lettuce and Brut. But whatever, even though there are millions of much cheaper used cars out there, in good nick and with all the seats pointing in the right direction, we still go for new. If the budget is tight though, your particular minefield will be extra full, because there really is some dross at the bottom of the automotive food chain.

Cars to go for:

Fiat Panda

You really cannot go wrong with this car – unless it goes wrong, which being Italian, is a possibility. If it does though, it'll probably be some electrical bonus thing, like a light, that you won't really miss. That aside, the latest Panda is yet more evidence that when they put their backs into it, no one can match the Italians for making cheap small cars. Inside it's roomy enough for any family practising Catholic birth control, and it's a laugh round corners, and there's even a button to make the steering lighter for town driving. That'll probably break though.

Citroën Berlingo

We love the Berlingo on *Top Gear*. It started out in life as a van, then got tarted up a bit with the addition of cloth seats, windows and buttons that make things happen electrically, but like the stubborn Frenchman that it is, the Berlingo still displays its van-ness with massive pride. There's bags of room, you don't have to be precious with the cargo area, it's quite nice to drive, cheap for a family car at ten grand, and as a massive bonus, its honesty makes it very, very cool.

Cars to avoid:

Perodua Kenari

Just look at it. There's more dignity to be had going to work on a space hopper. The journey would actually be nicer too, given that a space hopper is considerably more technologically advanced than this Malaysian wheelbarrow. A decent one, as in one with doors and an engine, costs around the same as a Fiat Panda, but the difference in quality is like the gap between a school play and the opening ceremony of the Olympics. And then we come to the looks: an egg box with head-lights just isn't that cool.

Daewoo Tacuma

Another orphan that hit every branch of the ugly tree on the way down. And just in case you're worrying that you might be faced with a dilemma – like, underneath that eyesore of a body there's a good car – then relax. Daewoo have simplified everything by making the car as bad to drive as it looks. A well-equipped one costs around twelve grand, which is much cheaper than, say, a Renault Scénic. But if you want cheap and new in this size, go for the Citroën Berlingo.

CITY WHIZZKID

This really applies to any business man or woman who, on the surface, has a lot going for them. You make money; your job involves deals, adrenalin, mirrored skyscrapers, power, ruthlessness, international phone calls, sharp suits, zinc bar tops, helicopters and à la carte menus. In decision-making you walk the razor's edge of a gambler, and the opposite sex is friendly. The trouble is, though, everyone and everything around you feels so good, so capitalistically positive, that you may not be aware that you're a bit of a cock. The big problem here is you have a need to go for the accessories that instantly let everyone know what a success you are, which in turn makes you a walking cliché. But there are cars which ooze style yet don't follow the herd.

Cars to go for:

Mercedes CLS

A bit of an oddball addition to the Mercedes line-up in that it has four doors, but it's called a coupé because it's so slinky at the back end. Confusing, but think of it as getting two extra doors for free, which should appeal to your business instincts. Like the Maserati, it will be a refreshingly rare sight around town, but unlike the Maserati it looks obviously beautiful.

Ferrari F430

We're assuming you can't possibly spend any more of your bonus on plasma tellys, so the F430, with its £100,000 plus price tag, should solve that headache. To be honest, it's not a cool car. Ferraris never are, but the 430 is so unbelievably good at its job, it will appeal to the 'maximum performance/survival of the fittest/close that deal' DNA in spades. Its technology crushes all rivals, with a 490-bhp V8 kept in check by acres of chassis computers. There's even an F1-style switch to operate it that's so big, you can point it out through the wine bar window.

Cars to avoid:

Toyota Avensis

You might be thinking of this because there was that advert on TV where some city boys play squash and then get in an Avensis and all fall silent in awe. That is truly a sparkling work of fiction. The only reason you'll fall silent in an Avensis is because there's nothing, and I mean nothing, to say about it. If you're really pushed, you could mention that the grille is ugly, but that's it. The rest of the Avensis is just a collection of metal, rubber, glass and plastic squashed together into a sort of car shape.

Saab 9-3

This car works well for other professions and lifestyles, but amongst the tribes of Gordon Gekko, it's just a bit, well, soppy. Have you ever been carved up, overtaken, or road raged by somebody in a Saab? Exactly. Do Saabs get used as getaway cars or for going dogging in? Exactly. Turning up in a Saab is giving out the message that you'll lose your nerve and sell low when the dollar is high or whatever it is that you shouldn't do. The same goes for the Toyota Prius, unless you're a futures broker who buys and sells tofu.

OLD PERSON IN EASTBOURNE

The grey pound is streaked with silver as far as car dealers are concerned. Nothing gets salesmen quivering more than the sight of two senior citizens approaching the showroom doors with a big bag of pension money to spend on a little treat for the twilight years. But a bewildering array of machinery awaits out there as the car market splinters into smaller and smaller sectors, so below are some handy hints to make life a little easier.

Cars to go for:

Mercedes SLK

This is the classic 'I've sacrificed lots to give my kids the best, now sod off and let me have some fun' car. It's a convertible, so perfect for those balmy promenade posing days, but it's also one of the new breed with a folding metal roof for when it becomes one of those promenade pissing-down days. It also looks stun-

ning and modern – the front end looks like an F1 car – so you don't come across as having given up. And best of all, for those who are hitting the Ralgex quite hard, the seats come with an 'air scarf' device which blows warm air on to your neck. Lovely.

Honda Accord

Hondas, as ever, are built with the structural integrity of anvils, and senior citizens admire this in a car. The new Accord retains this quality, but, thanks to its more modern looks, has shed some of the *Last of the Summer Wine* image that tends to afflict the brand. Where this car really scores, though, is as a long journey tourer. The ride is superb, and the 2.2-litre diesel engine, even though it's a first attempt for Honda, is up there with the best of them for quietness and speed. Never again will you tour the Dales in such style.

Cars to avoid:

Honda Civic Type R

From a bit of a distance it looks like a normal Honda Civic, which, as we know, is prime senior citizen transport. The Type R however is the hot hatch version, with 200-bhp and a 0–60 time of just 6.6 seconds. It is an amazing little sports car to drive, but unfortunately it's also an acquired taste, with a bone-crashingly hard ride and a noisy cabin – the wrong environment frankly, for the Archers. Beware though, because some scamp of a dealer may still try and sell you one. He might tell you the 'R' stands for 'Retired', just to get his hands on your sixteen grand. If he does, see him off with a karate chop.

Citroën Pluriel

As with the Honda, another trap lurks beneath the smooth salesroom banter. In essence the Pluriel is a cute little French car costing around twelve grand, and its party piece is the complex removable roof, which gives you many options for open-top travel, from sort of big sunroof status, to fully convertible. You may have visions of fantastic summer's-day excursions in search of mint cake, but beware: what isn't in the brochure is that the removable roof-supports weigh just slightly less than a tractor, and if you do take them off there's nowhere to store them, so you have to leave them behind, which is a pain, especially if you're planning on going to the shops via Bolivia.

GIRL ABOUT TOWN

The actual driving experience isn't the key issue here; most journeys will be just a mile or so spent staring up the pipe of the bus in front whilst drinking a frothy-mocha-skinny-latte-cappuccino and flicking through *Cosmo*. A dining chair with a moped engine could do the job. But the thing is, if you care so much about every aspect of your appearance, then why not treat the car as part of your outfit too? For starters, there is some real uncool rubbish out there, and men instinctively notice when a girl has put some thought into her wheels. So get it right, and preferably without appearing to care. A bit like that thing models do when they spend hours putting on make-up that looks like they're not wearing any make-up. Oh, and for crying out loud, please don't give it a name, however much you love it.

Cars to go for:

Audi A4 Cabriolet

Wow, they'll think you're Audrey Hepburn. The A4 cabriolet is a beautifully built, discreetly handsome luxury car. Boyfriends will love the build quality, your dad will go dizzy with pride, your mum will want to take you shopping in it and your

girlfriends will love you for ever and ever, or until the lease is up. A word of caution though: avoid the sporty S4 version – you'll look like you're trying too hard – and do not let them talk you into buying the diesel. Why would you want a glamorous convertible with a tractor engine? It's like buying a waterproof cocktail dress, or lingerie with tool loops.

350Z Roadster

The 350Z looks strong and purposeful, with a big 3.0-litre engine, rear wheel drive and a chunky leather interior, but it's easy to live with and should be endlessly reliable without the boring fragility of some sports cars. Best of all, blokes just roll over and go all giggly when they see a girl in a muscle car. You can blow their socks off in the pub by talking about how it continues the theme of the great Nissan Z cars of the seventies. Be warned though; it's fine when you talk about it, but if a bloke does, run away. He's a geek.

Cars to avoid:

Ford Fusion

Ford took a Fiesta and made it a bit taller for no reason that anyone has ever been able to determine. Unless you operate a service ferrying people into Ascot, you won't need the extra hat-room, so you would be better off with the standard Fiesta. Watch out, though. Salesmen will try and sell you one, so be warned. It's hopeless and you don't need one – in fact, write it on a card: 'I neither want nor need a Fusion, you sweaty little man.' Learn this and recite it as you walk into the showroom.

Peugeot 206CC

The folding metal roof is clever, it looks kind of cutesy and it's a two-seater, but hold on a moment. If you turn up at a party and someone is wearing exactly the same outfit, what do you do? Exactly, you get out of there sharpish; it's a disaster. So why risk doing exactly the same thing with your car? It was briefly fashionable, but then everyone had one. It went from haute couture to Top Shop and you don't want to be seen in one. All the women at the BBC drive them – enough said.

GANGSTER

A life of crime may mean you can avoid concerning yourself with some things – income tax, social responsibility and parking fines, for instance – but it doesn't get you out of worrying about your choice of wheels. The wrong car for a villain could prove disastrous, fatal even. It's no good having the prettiest of motors if it doesn't have the puff to keep you beyond the reach of the long arm of you know who. And you'll soon regret spending your ill-gotten on a Ferrari the first time you run out of a bank to find there's no room in the boot for the swag. But image is important too. You can't demand money with menace if everyone's laughing at your Daihatsu Copen. Just like everyone else, today's gangster has to be prepared to spend a little time considering which wheels will work for him or her if they're going to get the best from the car, and avoid the pitfalls that could turn a pleasure into a pain.

Cars to go for:

Chrysler 300C

It's not a perfect car: it doesn't go all that well nor sound as good as it should, despite that big 5.7-litre hemi V8. The interior feels cheap and the prudish traction control is annoying. But come on, it doesn't matter if it's made of cardboard

with marshmallow seats, just look at it. When this pulls up outside the snooker hall, you pay up. More presence than a dozen ex-boxers in dinner suits, you could send Dale Winton out in it to collect the protection money and he'd bring it back with interest.

Hummer H2

This is a bit obvious, in fact it's as subtle as a well-aimed baseball bat, but what do you expect here, poetry? The Hummer H2 has as much in common with the combat Hummer as Will Young with ol' Blue Eyes himself, but it really doesn't matter. When it comes down to it, the Hummer is a massive, scary thing. With blacked-out windows, it could be Big Dave at the wheel or Little Mo, but who's going to take the chance? The weight and barn door aerodynamics mean running costs are high, but hey, just have to get busy.

GANGSTER

Cars to avoid:

Hyundai Sonata

Big, sombre saloon cars generally work for gangsters; they project gravitas and intent. After all, you don't 'pay someone a visit' accompanied by a little guy in a clown's hat – you bring a really big bloke in a serious suit. However, it's not much use if the bloke turns out to be a professional tap dancer with a lisp. And so it is with the Hyundai. It lacks substance, feels flimsy and God help you if you ever have to hurry. It will fall to pieces and Plod will catch you sitting in the road holding a steering wheel and looking sheepish.

X-Type Jaguar

You're halfway there; a Jag is a good option for the gangster – think sixties villains in S-Types – but not this one. For a start, it looks too cuddly. Step out of this and you might as well replace your knuckledusters with feather ones, no one will take you seriously. Secondly, it's just a Mondeo with a picture of a cat on it. No gangster can afford to be seen to have had one put over on them. Drive this and everyone will know someone's pulled a fast one on you, namely Jaguar.

LOCAL CELEBRITY

With more and more television channels, digital radio stations and reality TV shows arriving by the minute, we are all headed for celebrity. But with fame, comes responsibility. Your image becomes more than a matter of personal vanity, your public will have expectations of you, it's important that you don't disappoint. So let's assume you've finally made it, after years of struggling as a weekend club DJ and part time egg-grader, you've got your weekly slot on Radio Blackburn. You have worked long and hard to achieve the fame that you secretly always knew was awaiting you. People are going to look at you in the street from now on, hopefully, and what you drive will say a lot about you.

Cars to go for:

Mercedes A-Class

Think about it; you're ringing the boss at Rochester Boilers to discuss their new corporate video. 'You'll be able to spot me', you can say, 'I'll be coming in a Mercedes.' Enough said as far as your client's concerned. He now thinks he's booked someone in Jonathan Ross's league. But the A-Class is also a very good car in its own right. It looks sharper than the last one and is a bit more sophisticated inside. The slightly-raised driving position will get you seen, and there's loads of room to fill it with signed photos and mugs with your name on.

Renault Modus

Renault's miniature MPV will be as happy ferrying all your free promotional CDs down to the car boot sale on a Sunday as it is scooting around town to open hairdresser's salons. There are sound financial reasons for choosing the Modus, too; you're bound to get a good deal from the local dealer for a celebrity car with your name sign-written on it. Make sure they use removable decals, though. Never good to pick up your date in a car with your name and 'Chugwell Motors' in lime green down the side.

Cars to avoid:

Peugeot 1007

This is a great little car: smart, modern and practical, with its clever sliding doors and interior panels that can be replaced when you're bored of the colour scheme. You can tell people that you could afford a bigger car but chose a small one because it's kinder to the environment and you do a lot of work for charity. But there is a huge problem: how can you have your name down the side of a car with sliding doors? Heaven knows what it will end up spelling when the doors are open.

Lamborghini Murcielago Roadster

In the old days, people walked up and asked for an autograph. Today, the mobile phone camera has replaced the autograph book. How will you feel the first time someone asks if they can take a photo and then asks you to move because you are obscuring the car? And think about it, with the roof down, at every set of traffic lights you will be able to hear them wondering who you are. Never buy a car that is a bigger star than you are, and, trust me, this one is.

IT CONSULTANT

The modern-day equivalent of going down the pit, the path to IT consultancy is worn bare by the passing slip-ons of a million young chaps (and they are mostly chaps) looking forward to a career of tutting over other people's digital messes and sharing hot gossip by the water cooler. The image of the IT consultant is not, shall we say, a sexy one. You need to tell the world that you are smart, sassy and technology friendly, but not a geek. The correct choice of car can really help here. Be warned, though. There are some dangerous traps out there, cars that call to the unwary IT consultant with siren allure, but that can savagely dash his Burton's-clad body against the rocks of public humiliation and derision.

Cars to go for:

Mazda RX8

Clever car, clever choice. The RX8 has many good points – the rotary engine makes for great pub talk and you will love the high-tech centre console. It looks like it's been lifted straight from an arcade in Tokyo. Where the RX8 really scores for the guys, though, is with its hidden four

doors. Your mates will love the sporty looks, but potential girlfriends will see the secret doors and spacious rear-seat accommodation as signs that inside this playful, boyish IT consultant there lurks a paid-up family man in a cardigan.

Citroën C4 Coupé

You like innovative things, gadgets make you flushed and itchy, you love grey plastic, you are, in fact, a natural-born Citroën buyer. The C4 Coupé will satisfy all your technical tastebuds with its directional headlamps and seat that vibrates if you wander across lanes on the motorway. Sure, some of it, well probably most of it, will stop working after a few hours, but by then you'll be bored of it anyway and hankering after the next gizmo – and at least you'll be left with a functional, economical car to play with, rather than just the box it came in.

Cars to avoid:

Audi A2

Don't be dazzled by the brushed aluminium surfaces and damped coat hooks; the A2 is a dreadful thing, overpriced and under-engined. It tells the world that you're too mean to buy a proper, full-sized Audi and that you have a secret passion for MPVs. The ride is awful and, worst of all (and this should really set your IT teeth grating), it's not actually that clever. It may have a look described at its launch as 'architectural' (and ever since as plain 'crap'), but

it never delivers on that futuristic image. It has an engine, four wheels and, for a small car, it's really quite cramped. Not really moving the concept on much, is it?

BMW 3-Series Compact

You wouldn't buy half a computer, would you? Or half a dog. So why buy half a BMW? It looks like a Greek hotel that you were building in instalments and ran out of money. Why not go the whole hog and get the base-spec 316, tell the world what a mean-spirited, soulless, empty suit you really are? It's like pitching up in Barbados out of season, just to say you were there. If you must spend money on a small BMW, buy a 1-Series, just don't foul your neighbourhood with one of these.

FARMER

It's a little-known fact, but there are still a few hardy folk out there using the countryside for farming. These people are hard-working, tough and resilient, and their vehicles need to be the same. They have to grow bacon trees and cultivate milk ponds, all of which means driving around in mud a lot and transporting smelly border collies over the hills. The right choice of car here isn't just a matter of style, it could be the difference between life or death.

Cars to go for:

Land Rover Defender

For many people, an off-road car *is* a Land Rover. It's not without good reason that this British stalwart is standard issue in the Forces and amongst farmers, mountain rescue, and genuine, rugged, outdoorsy types. It's evolved since first appearing in the 1950s, but not by all that much. Still a very, very basic car, the Defender keeps plodding on with the dogged determination of an old donkey, and a similar smell. Top spec versions come with air con, CD player, central locking and electric windows, but don't go thinking it's a luxury Landie. That would be like having a luxury mangle.

Suzuki Jimny

Don't be fooled by the toy-town looks. Blokes with beards, beer guts and sand ladders might scoff, but the little Jimny is a terrier; tiny, tough and built for a purpose. Where others use

heavy chassis, big engines and a brute-force approach to off-roading, the little Jimny relies on light weight and a buzzy little 1.3-litre engine to keep it skimming across the top of obstacles that would bog down many a heavyweight contender. Remember, Suzuki got into the off-road thing early on with their lightweight SJ in the 1960s, so they've got credibility on the brown stuff.

Cars to avoid:

BMW X3

The term 'off-road' isn't really precise enough; it could simply mean any smooth stretch of ripple-free tarmac that isn't technically a public highway. In which case, the 3-Series based 'off-roader' could probably cope quite well. If the term is taken to mean something with

obstacles bigger than, say a small stone or a puddle, then it's in trouble. The X3 possesses no more off-road ability than a dining table. It is, in fact, best left off the road altogether, in a skip.

Range Rover Sport

Don't be confused by this car. The original Range Rover had two doors and was probably the best thing a farmer could have with its unbelievable off-road ability, hose-down plastic interior and decent on-road manners. This also has two doors and a Range Rover badge, but is very different. It is the company's idea of a sports car, which at the best part of three tonnes, is surprising. The 4.2-litre supercharged engine overcomes the weight issue, but think of the fuel consumption. How can you possibly turn up to claim your subsidies in this thing? They'll be asking you for a loan.

ENVIRONMENTALIST

This is tricky. You love the planet, you recycle, you don't wear leather, you meditate and practise tai-chi. All excellent, laudable stuff, but you also have to get to work and bring home the tofu. It's a dilemma. How to drive a car without leaving an ugly skid-mark on Mother Nature's underpants? It's about more than emissions; you must consider how much fuel a car will consume and what resources are used in building and, eventually, recycling it. Be careful, there are some nasty customers out there – liars that will fool you with their gentle exteriors and pastel colours, only to be revealed as ravenous devourers of the planet.

Cars to go for:

Toyota Prius

The Prius was designed especially for you. It has two engines; whenever possible it relies on the clean-running electric motor, using the petrol one only when extra power is needed to go uphill or pull away. It even uses its own momentum when you're braking or going downhill to recharge the batteries, effectively recycling its own power. The result is a claimed 75 miles per gallon. But the important thing is, you'll pull in it. Sensitive types with poetry books in their duffel coats will swoon at your feet and pale-faced women in wholemeal sandals will offer you nutloaf treats.

Citroën C1

If you took one look at the tiny Citroën C2 in a showroom and thought it was too big, then this is the solution. Cars can't get much smaller than the C1 until people start shrinking. Not surprisingly, fuel consumption is minimal and the 1.4-litre diesel version will return around 65 mpg. Citroën claim it will accommodate four adults, but if they have all been at the sprout and lentil curry the night before, I'd rather not try it. This is a noble choice though, suited to someone of your convictions. If you collide with a hedgehog, it is you who will bravely bear the brunt of the impact, thus saving the creature.

Cars to avoid:

Citroën 2CV

The paper-thin, flimsy body uses hardly any of Mother Earth's precious resources. It is fantastically slow too. Even the doziest of potential road-kill will have time to spot you coming and saunter off without having to look like it's hurrying. But don't be fooled. Beneath that gently freckled, Waltons exterior, lurks a planet-killer with a soul as dark as pitch. That tiny two-cylindered engine was designed in the 1700s and built in factories by six-year-old chimney sweeps. Next time you see one, frown at it, hard.

Ford GT

It's very aerodynamic, so you shouldn't damage too much air, and the wedge shape will push hedgehogs aside without harming them even at speed. Unfortunately, it is a bit thirsty and can get down to just 6 miles to the gallon. Some owners have resorted to simply feeding it big chunks of oil-rich land rather than messing about extracting the min-

eral from it first. It saves time and the car seems to like it. 515 bhp and 200 mph won't impress anyone down at the yoga club either.

NEW MONEY LANDOWNER

The landed gentry might dress like rejects from a bad play and decorate their houses like seaside hotels, but they seem to know a thing or two about picking the right wheels. If you're going to fit in with the toffs, your car is probably the single biggest style decision you can make. Pitching up for the christening of the young Lord Blythe-Smythe-Fotherington in a gaudily modified Japanese sports car would be worse than vomiting into the font. The gentry treat their cars as they do their wax jackets and their furniture. They are only really fit to be seen once they are covered in dog hair and full of holes. They must look like they were once reasonably expensive but are now eternally on the point of disintegration and have never actually been new.

Cars to go for:

Land Rover Discovery

A Range Rover, unless it's a battered old beige one, might be seen as trying a bit too hard, so go for the less ostentatious but no less capable Discovery. It is possibly the best off-road car ever built thanks to a combination of clever technolo-

gy and rugged design. The flexible interior can easily accommodate seven drunken hoorays with the third row of seats set up, but you will struggle to get the sack of dead pheasants in the boot. Be warned, though; you will be first in the county to have one and eyebrows will be raised. But someone has to start the ball rolling and as long as you remember never to clean it, your chums will come to like the old warhorse.

Subaru Legacy Outback

Toffs love estate cars. The clue is in the word, 'estate'. The Subaru is everything close to a true blue-blood's heart; tough and resilient, well put together and best of all, completely discreet. Indeed, this side of a cloak of invisibility, nothing guarantees you the ability to go unnoticed more effectively than a Legacy Outback. With four-wheel drive and longer travel suspension, it will carry you and your picnic down to your lake with ease, and the 3-litre version is decently fast, without being vulgar. Being a Subaru, it will still be there long after the demise of socialism.

Cars to avoid:

BMW X5

A 4x4 can be acceptable amongst the upper classes, but only so long as it is green, down at heel and full of old shotgun cartridges and walking sticks. It is not acceptable to sweep up the gravel drive in a black BMW X5 with blacked-out windows and 22-inch chromed-alloy wheels. Park one of these on a street corner for more than

twenty seconds and thin young men with their hoods up will be tapping anxiously on the privacy glass and asking if they can score. You'll assume they're talking about keeping tally at a cricket match and make the most terrible ass of yourself.

Bentley Continental GT

Waiting for the man to bring the Bentley round has the right ring to it, but not if it's this one. Scratch any piece of furniture in a stately home and you will find more wood underneath. This is because the upper classes enjoy craftsmanship and all that goes with it. Scratch a Bentley Continental GT and you will find a VW lurking close to the surface. And then there's the problem of other owners: footballers, TV presenters with orange faces, and celebrity chefs as famous for their swearing as their cooking, are probably not the sort you want to see coming the other way in the same car as you.

SALES REP

This section applies basically to everyone at David Brent level and a bit below. Two things matter if you sell for a living: first, and most important, making an impression, and secondly, if you're on the road a lot, covering the miles in comfort. You also need plenty of kit for your money, then at least you'll have plenty of buttons to press when you're in a traffic jam. Overall, the best cars to go for are still the saloons and hatchbacks. Ultimately, the world of business is still a conservative one, and anyway, turning up in a family people carrier is just sort of wrong. You look like a parent who's got lost.

Cars to go for:

Golf GTi

Last year this would have been a big no-no. In fact, for the last twelve years now the Golf GTi has been a shadow of the original, as exciting as lettuce. But this year's model, the Mark 5, is the comeback kid. For a start it's got real power, a 2-litre 200-bhp turbocharged engine good for 145 mph, and even though it goes round corners with zest, it can still cover two hundred miles of motorway in comfort. It's not silly money at twenty grand, and finally, it looks the business with the alloys and its chunky front grille.

Peugeot 407 SW

In truth there are better cars around to drive, but this has been chosen for its looks. The SW, which is a nouvelle cuisine way of saying 'estate car', just has that air about it that says you've thought about your choice, that you've been intelligent, and in the car park at Deltron Systems Inc Worldwide PLC, it will merit a second glance as you step out. And even though it starts at £16,000, every model comes with air con. Go for the 1.6 diesel.

Cars to avoid:

Hyundai Sonata

This is one of Korea's prestige saloons, which is a bit like saying let me introduce you to one of Britain's friendliest VAT inspectors. If you're not bothered about image, ride, handling, performance, exterior looks or interior looks, then this is the car for you. You might be tempted because of the price – the V6 auto, after all, is only seventeen grand, but when you have to sit day after day, in a jam, wondering why the fake wood trim doesn't even look like fake plastic, you'll regret your miserliness. Even a debt collector up north wouldn't drive this car.

Ariel Atom

A truly great car if your day job is testing rollercoasters, but for stationery salesmen it does have one or two drawbacks. The lack of a roof is a big one. And doors, because the car's amazing skeletal structure means for once the police will be able to see you doing your expenses in the outside lane, whilst you're also on the phone and unwrapping a Ginsters. Also, you'll arrive at appointments with your hair looking like it's been cut by piranhas, and gravel where your eyes once were. Shame. Great car.

COMPANY BOSS

Bosses aren't the miserable old goats they used to be in the 1970s. It's a combination of things, really. The technology revolution has stirred up the entrepreneur pot, socialism isn't the formidable enemy of capitalism it once was, and these days it's also OK to flash your wealth, as footballers prove in *Heat* magazine every week. All this means you can relax about coming through the gates in a nice car, but you've still got to get it right. Those in your workforce who like cars will analyse your choice carefully and believe me, they'll draw a moustache on your picture if they have no respect for your choice. Also, you can't be too conservative. How much of a visionary will you look if you turn up in yet another Jaguar?

Cars to go for:

Audi A6

Mercedes are too dull, Jaguars are too nostalgic, BMWs are too common – it's all leading in one direction, and that's to the Audi showroom. If a prestige German car is your weapon of choice, and for many it will be, then the Audi A6 has no equal. It may not drive as well as a BMW or a Jaguar, but it's the classiest-looking and without a shadow of a doubt it's the coolest. It says you are a stylish, possibly even caring, boss. The interior is superb, second only to the Range Rover's, and every detail, even down to the graphics on the in-car computer, is exquisitely designed. The V6 diesel is every engine you'll ever need.

Aston Martin AMV8

This car was made for bosses. It's a classic example of how to splash out many pounds on a fancy car, and yet retain the respect of even the most Trotskyite member of your workforce.

The thing is, this AMV8, the 'cheap' Aston, at around £80,000, is a direct rival for, say, a Porsche 911, but to some folks '911' is still the number of the beast, the beast being Thatcher. Astons, however, are loved by absolutely everybody, even lefties. On top of that you'll have a truly beautiful and rapid V8-powered car, and your secretary will think you're a secret agent and change her name to Moneypenny, which is your problem.

Cars to avoid:

Peugeot 607

In truth, the French haven't made a decent big car since the Citroën DS, but whereas most countries these days are content to leave this task to the Germans, the French, ploughing their own stubborn furrow as ever, still keep giving it a go. Their latest dismal offering is the Peugeot 607, which has been tarted up of recent with some new suspension, more in-car gizmos and a new facelift, but lookswise, it still belongs in the Ming dynasty. The cabin boasts real wood, but having gone to that trouble, they've still pulled off the amazing feat of making it look like plastic.

The difference between this car and an Audi is like the difference between Kate Moss and Jodie Marsh. They both have 'model' written in their passport, but you know what I mean.

Vauxhall Signum

On paper this is a proper executive car, in that the star features of the Signum are the huge rear seats and the rear leg room, which alone is vast enough to host a show-jumping event. The implication here is that the owner will be driven, but just ask yourself: if you're successful enough to be able to afford a chauffeur, you're hardly going to waste his talents on a twenty grand puffed-up Vauxhall Vectra estate are you? If you buy this, your workforce will lose faith and walk out, the shareholders will laugh, and the stock market will plummet, and then, just as your house is being repossessed, your chauffeur will sue for mental cruelty. You've been warned.

MEDIA TYPE

This category covers a whole host of professions – advertising, public relations, design, publishing, music industry, fashion, television, newspapers – and it's populated by people who truly believe their job is the most important in the world, even though it's not. Alongside this inbuilt arrogance, other common traits are pressure and deadlines, which all adds to a sense of drama, and the need to be perceived to be cutting edge, to be ahead of the game, which all adds to the sense of theatre. The visual messages you give off are vital for this last part, which means you cannot falter in your choice of car.

Cars to go for:

BMW M6

For starters, it's a coupé, which will appeal to all the forty-somethings trying to impress twenty-somethings. It's also a very handsome one, but challengingly handsome, with some ugly traits woven into the bodywork, and this will spark debate, which again is an important ritual in media life. The M6 is also a proper car for the enthusiast, with the extraordinary five-litre, 507-bhp V10 from the BMW M5 under the bonnet, and more Formula One-style computing power in the gearbox

and engine than in any other road car. This last point makes the car cutting-edge modern, which is crucial, and yet the whole package is very discreet, so you won't offend Stella McCartney or any other vegetarians on Planet Media.

Renault Mégane

The BMW costs a lot – around £70,000 – but for those working their way up the ladder, you'll find plenty of cheap chic in a Renault Mégane. In truth, there are better-built hatchbacks around that are more exciting to drive, but not one of them comes close to the Renault for the sheer boldness of its looks. And amazingly, for something so extreme, it's a look that ages well. Your Mégane must be black, or deep blue, and it must be three-door. For those who worry about the world's resources, the diesel engines are good, and £14,000 will get you a nice version loaded with toys, including an ignition key shaped like a credit card. Just don't try and use it in Harvey Nichols.

Cars to avoid:

Porsche Cayenne

It may have the Porsche badge, the Porsche performance and the Porsche engineering, but at heart this is a fashion car, bought to impress, and if you're buying one now, you've missed the boat and you ain't impressing anyone but your dealer. There's another problem too. This is a huge off-roader, but because the stylists at Porsche are only capable of making one shape, as they've been proving with the 911 for the last forty years, they've tried to make the Cayenne look a bit like a 911. And the result is ugliness. But not ugliness you can chew over the merits of with an architect; just plain, old-fashioned, not much use to anyone, ugliness.

Ford Fiesta ST

Fast Fords are held in reverence by lots of car lovers, because they brought power to the people, which makes for a nice story – a film script even, with a soundtrack and publicity campaign. And now there's a hot Fiesta back in town with a perky engine, 150 bhp, and sharp handling to match. It's quick, precise and modern – just like you, but it's also loved by Chavs, which is not you. This car is destined for a life of owners wearing Burberry check, so avoid.

FIGHTER PILOT

In reality this section is for anyone who feels the need for speed, but fighter pilots have been singled out for special attention because despite the fact that these chiselled warriors defend the skies at mach 3 whilst we sleep safely in our beds, they always seem to choose rubbish cars. The chief instructor at the British equivalent of the Top Gun school, for example, has an old Volvo estate. What message would that have sent out to Jerry in 1940? The cars featured here are also aimed at the non-family man. If you are a fighter pilot who's not firing blanks and want a five-seater with fire in its belly, please refer to the chapter on Family Cars.

Cars to go for:

Vauxhall Monaro VXR

What we have lurking behind the Vauxhall badge is a big muscle car from Australia. Cars, like the people, are simple down there, and this is no exception. It's rear-wheel drive, there's plenty of power from the 5.7-litre V8 – almost 380 bhp in fact – and in contrast to the bewildering array of cockpit buttons in your Harrier, you

get just two settings for the traction control: on or off. That's actually all you need though, because it's fantastically easy to drive, loves going round bends, and if you do have a bit of a moment with the back end, it'll all gather nice and safely without putting you in a flat spin. It's also loaded with kit, and for £35,000 it's hard to find more car for the money.

Vauxhall VX 220 Turbo

In terms of hard-core sports cars, it's a toss-up between this and the Lotus Exige. Both have that fit-for-purpose menacing look about them, both are phenomenally good at taking a twisty B road and clubbing it into submission, and in a straight line, either car will have a good go at punching through the sound barrier. Either one is a spiritual successor to the 1940s MG with the labrador in the back, but of the two, go for the Vauxhall. It's three grand cheaper at £26,000, more user-friendly in everyday life, and with a 0–60 time of sub-five seconds, you'll still be Top Gun when it's chocks away at the lights.

Cars to avoid:

Daihatsu Copen

If you see a picture of this car, just don't be fooled into thinking: 'Mmmm, nice nimble Japanese roadster, just the job.' In the flesh it's only a bit bigger than a chocolate orange, and no man, apart from perhaps an interior decorator called Jermaine, who's locked in a love triangle with John Inman and Graham Norton, could possibly be seen in it. Certainly not Biggles. If you're picked up on enemy satellite driving this, our shores will be invaded by nightfall.

Skoda Fabia VRS

The Fabia is immaculately built under the watchful eye of its Volkswagen owners, and the VRS version really is quite quick. It can put down its power without altering the shape of the world's tectonic plates. But think what you're doing. You land your fighter at one of those air shows, climb down from the cockpit and stroll, in a heat haze, teeth flashing, towards the applauding crowd. And then you pull out a Skoda key ring to open your car. Think what you're doing. There are children watching and they'll be traumatised by such a sight. Skodas may

be better than they were, but they're for people who read *Which?* and write to *Points of View*, not heroes who look for bandits at six o'clock.

CONCLUSION

Now you've got to this bit, we hope that you read the rest of the book first, and if you have, thank you. Now don't forget to wash your hands.

We hope you've enjoyed it, and more importantly that you've picked up the key facts: you can ruin your marriage by pitching up at the church in the wrong car; if you get a classic wrong by just an inch, you've missed by a mile; this week's fashion car could be next week's fashion disaster; and you don't have to give up when you buy a family car. Overall, what we're saying is that, in order to cope with all the major events in life, you should plan to have a garage of about eight to ten cars. To do that, you will need to be earning about £500,000 a year. After tax. So crack on then.

PICTURE ACKNOWLEDGEMENTS

Auto Express Picture Library (special thanks to Danielle Geraghty).
5, 8 12, 16, left above right, 17, 18 above, 19 above & below, 20–23 left, 24 below left, 25 below, 26 left, 40–44, 46, 48–53 above, 54–57, 59–60 above, 62 left, 63 left, 64 right, 67 above, 71 above, 72–73 below left & below right, 74–75, 79 right, 81, 89 centre, 92 below, 99 right, 100–101, 103–104, 106–107, 109–115, 117, 120–121, 123–125, 127–129, 131–133, 135 below, 139–140, 142–146, 149–150, 152–157.

Car and Bike Photo Libraries (special thanks to David Kimber).
16 below, 17 below, 18 below, 23 right, 24 above right, 25 above right, 28, 30, 32, 33–35, 37, 47, 53 below, 60 below, 61, 64 left, 65–66 left, 73 above, 79 above left & below left, 84–89 above & below, 90–92 above, 93, 95, 108, 118, 126, 130, 136–138, 141, 147, 148, 151.

Getty Images 38.

Newspress Ltd 45, 67 below, 105.

Rex Features (special thanks to Stephen Atkinson).
Front and back endpapers. 3, 4, 6, 7, 9–12 (inset), 13, 15, 24 below right, 25 above left, 26 right, 27, 31, 62 right, 63 above right, 66 right, 71 below, 76–77, 82, 99 left, 119, 135 above.